*ORACLE*

*SQL*

*&*

*PL/SQL*

# *Performance Tuning*

(N. Gupta)

# Table of Contents

# About SQL and SQL Tuning

## Need for SQL Tuning

Tuning of database can be a difficult task, most particularly when you are working with large number of data. Sometimes in Oracle database we might need to run some queries which can take lot of time. The obvious reason behind long time taking is very large sized tables which have millions and millions of records. So ultimately we need to do tuning to SQL queries which can reduce the time taken to execute the query.

SQL tuning involves re-writing (changing) the SQL statement in a manner which helps in retrieving the results of the query in a faster and more efficient manner, without hampering the original functionality of the statement.

Tuning is basically an activity which helps to increase the performance of a system. It allows to get the best throughput or response time and thus make the best use of the available resources.

Tuning can be done at both the code (SQL and/or PLSQL tuning) or in the database (DBA tuning –memory, tables etc.).

When we query the database we get the data needed. The SQL query processing however happens in a step by step process as given below

1. The input query is processed by a query parser which checks for keywords, column names, table names and the syntax. Once these are valid, the parser produces a query tree.

2. The query tree is a logical plan of execution in the form of algebraic expressions. An optimizer prepares a physical plan of execution using the query tree, by choosing an access path which is considered to be most optimized.

3. The execution plan is later executed in the form of machine code to provide the output.

## Understand the execution of the SQL query

The following figure shows the phases in sql query execution.

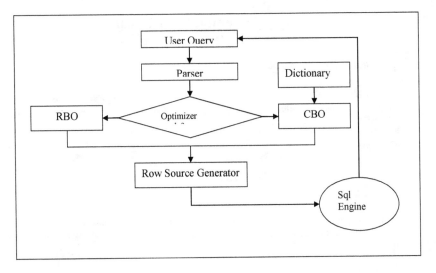

**Parser:**
     Check the syntax and semantics in the query.

**Optimizer:**
     The optimizer uses internal rules or costing method to determine the most efficient way of producing the results of the query.

**Row Source Generator:**
     The Row source generator retrieves the optimal execution plane (tree structure) from the optimizer and passes it to sql execution engine to execute the query based on the optimal plan.

**SQL Execution Engine:**
     The sql execution engine executes the query using the optimal execution plan from the row source generator and produces the result to the user.

# Basic Tuning for SQL Query

## Ordering of the FROM clause.

When we are fetching data from more than one table, write the table with fewer rows at the end of the FROM clause. Therefore, the table returning the least number of rows should be last in the FROM list.

**Example:**

*SELECT COL1 FROM TAB1, TAB2, TAB3*
*WHERE VAL = 'ABC';*

In the above query the no. of rows present in TAB1 is maximum, followed by TAB2 and TAB3 contains the least rows. Therefore, order of arranging tables in FROM clause is TAB1, TAB2 and then TAB3

## Disabling use of indexes

Generally indexed are disabled inadvertently due to modification of column data type.

**Example:**

*SELECT INC_AMT FROM TAB1*
*WHERE TO_CHAR (TRAN_ID) = '1234';*

The reason for this is that oracle cannot use an index if the column is modified in the where clause. It is up to the developer to ensure that, WHERE clause columns, aren't modified in any way.

Below query will also stop the usage of index

*SELECT INC_AMT FROM TAB1*
*WHERE TRAN_ID + 1 = 1234;*

**Correct usage:**

*SELECT INC_AMT FROM TAB1*
*WHERE TRAN_ID = '1234';*

## Use of ! = operator

Unless it is absolutely necessary, avoid using the! = operator. The use of this operator disables the use of indexes, because Oracle assumes that the query will be retrieving most of the rows in the table. This operator results in a Full table scan which can be lead to serious performance issues if the table size is large.

## Index Rule

Only use indexes for retrieving data from tables, where your want less than 20 percent of the rows. Full table scans are quicker if you want more than 20 percent of a table's data.

## INSERT using *

Although the use of the character '*' is allowed by the oracle, it is considered to be bad programming practice and hence it should be avoided.

## Resource intensive operations

Queries, which use DISTINCT, UNION, MINUS, INTERSECT, ORDER BY and GROUP BY clause upon Oracle to perform resource intensive sorts. Generally, these operators cause a full table scan. Re-writing SQL query without these operators using other alternative approaches is the best way.

## Avoiding unnecessary joins

SQL is a very expressive language and there are normally several ways of performing the same query. Developers should investigate different wordings of the same query, so as to identify the optimal query.

Below query can be written in multiple ways

**Example 1:**

```
SELECT TAB2.INC_AMT FROM TAB1, TAB2
WHERE TAB1.COL1 = TAB2.COL1
AND TAB1.FLG='Y';
```

**Example 2:**

```
SELECT TAB2.INC_AMT
  FROM TAB2
WHERE TAB2.COL1 IN (SELECT TAB1.COL1
       FROM TAB1
             WHERE TAB1.FLG ='Y');
```

Example 2 executed in a less time and plan cost is lower than example 1. Avoiding unnecessary joins is a good SQL practice. Therefore, example 2 is an optimal way of writing the above query.

## Problem with Implicit type conversion / using functions on Indexed columns.

In Oracle, the same Information stored in different data type columns in two tables. E.g. the PO Line Id in PO_Lines table is "number", whereas the same Line_id is stored in PK1_Value (Varchar2) in Fnd_Attached_Documents table. So, if we need to join these tables with this criterion, we are comparing "varchar2" with "Number". In these cases, oracle uses implicit conversion of data types and leads to full table scan.

## Use Table Aliases:

Use table aliases to address tables when more than one table present in FROM clause. It will reduce the parser's work. In addition, avoids the confusion, as same column name may exist in more than one table. Later a column with the same name added to other table and table aliases will prevent the column ambiguity.

> *SELECT emp.emp_no,emp.emp_name,emp.dept_no*
> *FROM employee emp, Department dept*
> *WHERE dept.dept_no = emp.dept_no;*

## Use EXISTS in the place of IN

Whenever an outer query check a presences of some records in an inner query then use EXISTS with it. IN option in a query will give a full table scan. It will affect the performance of a query when huge records present in the table.

E.g. select customer details, who are all also a members of a club

> *SELECT cust.cno,cust.cname,cust.addr*
> *FROM customer cust*
> *WHERE exists (Select * from club Where cno = cust.cno)*

Also use NOT EXIST instead of NOT IN because NOT IN cannot use indexes.

## Ordering Table in FROM clause

Arrange the tables in the right end of FROM clause in such a way that:

1. The table which has least number of rows
2. The table to which input conditions applied
3. The table which has more joins in WHERE clause

The table in the right end of the FROM clause is called **driving table**.

## Use '>=, <=' operators instead of BETWEEN

The BETWEEN operator will be converted to '<= and >=' internally this will affect the execution time of the query.

## Use of GROUP BY and ORDER BY

Filter all the possible conditions in the WHERE clause instead of using HAVING clause.
In addition, do not use ORDER BY clause whenever you are using UNION, MINUS, DISTINCT or GROUP BY kind of features because these queries will be in sorted form in ascending order.

## UNION and UNION ALL

When use more than one UNION in a query, use UNION ALL for all the queries and UNION for last join of the query.

# Oracle Hints

Optimizer will choose the best plan by using CBO or RBO techniques. Oracle also allows user to force the optimizer to execute the query in a given way by using the hints.

This is the interesting topic for controlling Execution plan through SQL hint. Oracle generally uses optimizer that optimize query execution plan. If Optimizer is doing a good job then SQL hint is not needed. But in real life scenario, Characteristics of Data is changing rapidly so that optimizer may be out of date. In this case, there are some SQL hints which really help to change execution plan so that query executes faster.

Syntax:      Select /*+ hint */
             Select /*+ hint (argument1) */
             Select /*+ hint (argument1 argument2) */

All hints uses CBO except /*+ rule */. No Schema names should be used in Hints. It should contain only alias name if the alias is used for the table.
There are hundreds of documented and undocumented hints. We'll see only the important hints which is really helps Performance tuning.

Syntax:

    SELECT /*+ Hint1 Hint2...Hintn*/ column_list
        FROM table_list
        WHERE conditions;

We can set the optimizer mode through hints like,

    SELECT /*+ first_rows_10 */ column_list
        FROM table_list
        WHERE conditions;

Oracle supports many hints to tune a sql query some of them are,

| Hints | Example |
|-------|---------|
| FULL | Explicitly choose full table scan for a specified table.<br><br>SELECT /*+ FULL(emp) */ *<br>FROM emp<br>WHERE emp_id = 1; |
| APPEND and NOAPPEND | APPEND: Will append the data in the table without using default space allocated to the table. Also it will not create UNDO |

| | |
|---|---|
| | NOAPPEND: Will insert data in conventional INSERT by disabling parallel mode for the duration of the INSERT statement.<br><br>INSERT /*+ *APPEND* */ INTO t<br>    SELECT *<br>    FROM all_objects<br>        WHERE SUBSTR(object_name,1,1)<br>    BETWEEN 'C' AND E; |
| CURSOR_SHARING_EXACT | Oracle optimizer used to convert the literals to bind variables. This replacement can be controlled by the CURSOR_SHARING parameter.<br>CURSOR_SHARING_EXACT hint will instruct the optimizer to switch off this behavior.<br><br>SELECT /*+ *CURSOR_SHARING_EXACT* */ * FROM emp WHERE emp_id = 101; |
| INDEX | Instruct the optimizer to use the index to perform the query.<br><br>SELECT /*+ *INDEX(emp ind_gen)* */ *<br>FROM emp<br>WHERE gender = F; |
| INDEX_COMBINE | Instruct the optimizer to use the bitmap combination.<br>If no arguments passed to this hint then optimizer will take any best combination of Boolean bitmap indexes.<br><br>SELECT /*+ *INDEX_COMBINE(e ind_mgr ind_dept))* */ *<br>  FROM employees e<br>WHERE (manager_id = 80 OR<br>     department_id = 310); |
| INDEX_ASC and INDEX_DESC | Explicitly choose index scan with ascending or descending order of the index values based on the hints. |
| INDEX_FFS | Instruct the optimizer to go for fast full index scan rather than a full table scan |
| LEADING | With the help of this hint we can tell oracle to use the specified table as the ruling or first table in the join order. More in technical way we can say that LEADING hint will instruct the optimizer to utilize the mentioned tables as prefix in the execution plan.<br>This hint will be ignored if the tables mentioned cannot be joined in the order specified. For example:<br>*SELECT /*+ LEADING (a, b) */ * FROM customers a, departments t, history_job b*<br>*WHERE a.dept_id=t.dept_id AND a.hired_dt=b.started_dt* |

| | |
|---|---|
| USE_HASH | This hint will request for a hash join between the mentioned tables. Hash join is basically a technique where Oracle loads the data/rows from the driving table (the first table after the where clause) into the RAM. Oracle then uses a hashing technique to locate the rows in the larger second table. For example : <br><br> *SELECT /\*+ USE_HASH(a,b) \*/ a.name, b.com FROM sup a, bonus b WHERE a.name = b.name* |
| USE_NL | This hint will request for a nested loop join, using the specified table as the inner table. In nested loop join oracle what does is that it reads the first row from the driving table also technically known as first row source and then searches the inner table (second row source) for matches. All matches are planted in a result set. This iteration/loop will continue till its processes all rows of the driving table. <br> For example : <br> *SELECT /\*+ USE_NL(a,b) \*/ a.cust_name, b.sup_name FROM customer a, supplier b WHERE a.customer_id = b.supplier_id* |

# SQL Join Condition

Joins in query used to combine more than one table and fetch required records.

Whenever we join more than one table, oracle must use one of the following options

- Nested loop join
- Hash join
- Sort merge join
- Cartesian join

## Nested loop joins

The optimizer uses nested loop joins when joining small number of rows, with a good driving condition between the two tables. It drives from the outer loop to the inner loop. The inner loop is iterated for every row returned from the outer loop, ideally by an index scan. It is inefficient when join returns large number of rows (typically, more than 10,000 rows is considered large), and the optimizer might choose not to use it.

The cost is calculated as below.
Cost = access cost of A + (access cost of B * no_of_rows from A)

a nested loop join involves the following steps:

1. the optimizer determines the driving table and designates it as the outer table.
2. The other table is designated as the inner table.
3. For every row in the outer table, Oracle accesses all the rows in the inner table.

For instance:

SELECT emp.empno, dept.dname
FROM EMP , DEPT
WHERE dept.deptno = 10
AND emp.deptno = dept.deptno


EMPNO DNAME
---------- ---------------
7782 ACCOUNTING
7839 ACCOUNTING
7934 ACCOUNTING

Execution Plan

```
------------------------------------------------------------
0 SELECT STATEMENT Optimizer=CHOOSE (Cost=3 Card=5 Bytes=85)
1 0 NESTED LOOPS (Cost=3 Card=5 Bytes=85)
2 1 TABLE ACCESS (BY INDEX ROWID) OF 'DEPT' (Cost=1 Card=1 Bytes=10)
3 2 INDEX (UNIQUE SCAN) OF 'PK_DEPT' (UNIQUE)
4 1 TABLE ACCESS (FULL) OF 'EMP' (Cost=2 Card=5 Bytes=35)
```

We can also force the Nested loop join hint as below.

```
SELECT /*+ USE_NL(emp dept) */ emp.empno, dept.dname
FROM EMP , DEPT WHERE dept.deptno = 10
AND emp.deptno = dept.deptno
```

### Hash Joins

Hash joins are used for joining large data sets. The optimizer uses the smaller of two tables or data sources to build a hash table on the join key in memory. It then scans the larger table, probing the hash table to find the joined rows. This method is best used when the smaller table fits in available memory. The optimizer uses a hash join to join two tables if they are joined using an equijoin (joins with equal's predicates) and large amount of data needs to be joined.

The cost of a Hash loop join is calculated by the following formula:
cost=(access cost of A*no_of_hash partitions of B) + access cost of B

For instance:

```
SELECT emp.empno, dept.dname
FROM EMP , DEPT
WHERE emp.deptno = dept.deptno
```

Execution Plan
```
------------------------------------------------------------
0 SELECT STATEMENT Optimizer=CHOOSE (Cost=5 Card=14 Bytes=238)
1 0 HASH JOIN (Cost=5 Card=14 Bytes=238)
2 1 TABLE ACCESS (FULL) OF 'DEPT' (Cost=2 Card=7 Bytes=70)
3 1 TABLE ACCESS (FULL) OF 'EMP' (Cost=2 Card=14 Bytes=98)
```

We can also force the Hash join hint as below:

```
SELECT /*+USE_HASH(emp dept) */ emp.empno, dept.dname
FROM EMP , DEPT
WHERE emp.deptno = dept.deptno
```

## Sort-Merge Join

Sort merge joins can be used to join rows from two independent sources. Hash joins generally perform better than sort merge joins. On the other hand, sort merge joins can perform better than hash joins if both of the following conditions exist:

1. The row sources are sorted already.
2. A sort operation does not have to be done.

Sort merge joins are almost exclusively used for non-equi joins (>, <, BETWEEN). Sort merge joins perform better than nested loop joins for large data sets. (You cannot use hash joins unless there is an equality condition). In a merge join, there is no concept of a driving table.
The join consists of two steps:
Sort join operation: Both the inputs are sorted on the join key.
Merge join operation: The sorted lists are merged together.

The optimizer can choose a sort merge join over a hash join for joining large amounts of data if any of the following conditions are true:

1. the join condition between two tables is not an equi-join.
2. OPTIMIZER_MODE is set to RULE.
3. HASH_JOIN_ENABLED is false.
4. Because of sorts already required by other operations, the optimizer finds it is cheaper to use a sort merge than a hash join.
5. The optimizer thinks that the cost of a hash join is higher, based on the settings of HASH_AREA_SIZE and SORT_AREA_SIZE.

The cost of a sort merge join is calculated by the following formula:
cost = access cost of A + access cost of B + (sort cost of A + sort cost of B)

```
SELECT emp.empno, dept.dname
FROM EMP , DEPT
WHERE emp.deptno < dept.deptno
```

Execution Plan
--------------------------------------------------------
```
0 SELECT STATEMENT Optimizer=CHOOSE (Cost=6 Card=5 Bytes=85)
1 0 MERGE JOIN (Cost=6 Card=5 Bytes=85)
2 1 SORT (JOIN) (Cost=2 Card=7 Bytes=70)
3 2 TABLE ACCESS (BY INDEX ROWID) OF 'DEPT' (Cost=2 Card=7 Bytes=70)
4 3 INDEX (FULL SCAN) OF 'PK_DEPT' (UNIQUE) (Cost=1 Card =7)
5 1 SORT (JOIN) (Cost=4 Card=14 Bytes=98)
6 5 TABLE ACCESS (FULL) OF 'EMP' (Cost=2 Card=14 Bytes=98)
```

We can also force the Hash join hint as below:

```
SELECT /*+USE_MERGE(emp dept) */
emp.empno, dept.dname
FROM EMP , DEPT
WHERE emp.deptno < dept.deptno
```

## Cartesian Join

A Cartesian join is used when one or more of the tables does not have any join conditions to any other tables in the statement. The optimizer joins every row from one data source with all the row from the other data source, creating the Cartesian product of the two sets.

For instance:

*Select \* from emp,dept;*

Execution Plan

```
-----------------------------------------------------------
0 SELECT STATEMENT Optimizer=CHOOSE (Cost=16 Card=98 Bytes=5194)
1 0 MERGE JOIN (CARTESIAN) (Cost=16 Card=98 Bytes=5194)
2 1 TABLE ACCESS (FULL) OF 'DEPT' (Cost=2 Card=7 Bytes=112)
3 1 BUFFER (SORT) (Cost=14 Card=14 Bytes=518)
4 3 TABLE ACCESS (FULL) OF 'EMP' (Cost=2 Card=14 Bytes=518)
```

# SQL Indexes

In general, "What's an index?" It's basically same like books/novels having index page. So that you don't have to scan through whole book to find whatever you are searching, you just have to scan through the index page and from there you can go directly to the page which you want to search.

So in Oracle database world, index is like a pointer which points to data, it's basically a lookup table which database search engine uses for fast retrieval of data. Indexes speeds up select queries and where clauses, but it also has a con i.e. it slows down data input which we do with UPDATE and INSERT statements. They can be created and dropped with no effect on core data as they are mutually exclusive.

## Types of Indexes

1. Single–Column Indexes – Created for only one column of a table.
2. Unique Indexes – The benefit of using unique index is that it does not allow duplicate data to be inserted into the table.
3. Composite Indexes – This can be created for multi columns.
4. Implicit Indexes – These are automatically created by database servers when objects like primary key constraints or unique constraints are created.

## On what occasions we should avoid indexes?

1. On small tables we should not use indexes.
2. Tables on which there is frequent bombardment of update/insert statements.
3. Columns containing higher number of NULL values.
4. Columns which are frequently changed should not be indexed.

An index is a performance tuning method to retrieve records faster. By default, Oracle creates b-tree index on unique column.

**Syntax:**

> CREATE [UNIQUE|BITMAP] INDEX index_name
> ON table_name (column1, column2... column_n)
> [COMPUTE STATISTICS];

Indexes cannot be used in the following situations,

- Columns that are updated frequently

- When there is no "where" clause in the query or the indexed column is not present in the "where" clause

- When search for NULL or NOT NULL in the query.
- Columns used only with functions and expressions.

We can use the following types of indexes in oracle,

1. B-tree index
2. Bitmap index
3. Function-based index

## Selectivity ratio

The selectivity ratio for choosing index is,

*Ratio = [NDV/NR]*

*NDV – Number of Distinct Values in the table column*

*NR – Number of Rows in the table.*

When the selectivity ration comes down 60% it's better to take Bitmap index and more than 60%, we can choose b-tree index.

## B-tree index

B-tree indexes are useful on the columns, which has more distinct values (High Cardinality) like emp_no, dept_no, etc. like as primary key index.

**Syntax:**

*CREATE INDEX name_ind ON table_name (column_names)*

The structure of the b-tree index is,

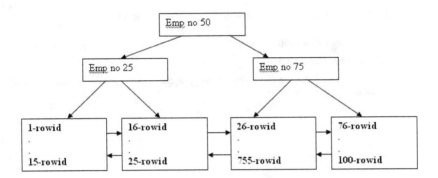

## Bitmap index

- Bitmap indexes are useful on the columns, which have less distinct values (less cardinality) like gender, manager_id, etc.,
- Bitmap indexes are stored efficiently. It requires less memory comparing to the B-tree indexes.
- RBO does not consider using bitmap indexes
- A Bitmap index uses the 0 and 1 to indicate whether the bitmap index condition is satisfied by the row or not. 1 indicate, the row satisfies the bitmap condition and 0 indicate, the row not satisfies the bitmap condition.

**Syntax:**

*CREATE BITMAP index name_ind ON table_name (column_names)*

The Bitmap indexes will use two-dimensional array to store the index values.

## Function-based index

Oracle provides feature to create index on functions either built-in functions or user functions. Optimizer will not use index for an indexed column when we use functions on the indexed column like to_char (emp_no) = '101'. We can create function-based index on the column for the function to make the optimizer to use the index on the column.

**Syntax:**

*CREATE INDEX name_ind ON table_name (fun_name(column_name))*

## Composite Indexes

The following points are useful when creating a composite index.

- Place the most queried columns first.
- Place most restrictive column first.
- Add the extra columns to the index so that you can retrieve the query result without accessing the base table.

# SQL Explain Plan

## EXPLAIN PLAN

Whenever user executes a query, oracle performs many steps. Each of these steps either retrieves data physically from the database or prepare in some other manner.
The combination of these steps to execute a statement is called execution plan.

Oracle execution plan contains the access-path for each table (to access the table) and ordering of the tables with appropriate joining method.

**Access-path**: It represents the number of units of work required to get data from a base table.

## Prerequisites to view the execution plan

The AUTOTRACE facility is an easier way to see the execution plan of a statement. This facility is in SQL*Plus. To use this facility we need to perform the following operations:

Run the script utlxplan.sql present in the path ORACLE_HOME/rdbms/admin/utlxplan.sql which creates the PLAN_TABLE.

The role PLUSTRACE is created by running the script plustrce.sql present in the path ORACLE_HOME/sqlplus/admin/plustrce.sql.

PLUSTRACE role must then be granted to the schema in which we need to perform the tuning of the SQL statements.

Execute the command "set autotrace on" which shows the execution plan of once the DML's statements are executed

To gather statistics, oracle provides great features like,

- Explain plan
- Sql plus AUTOTRACE
- Trace (Tkprof)

Using these features, we can get the statistics for the sql statements to analyze the performance of the statements.

## Create plan table

The script utlxplan.sql is used to create the plan table. The command is,

*@ utlxplan.sql*

The script is will be present in the path,
*Windows: %ORACLE_HOME%\rdbms\admin*
*Unix: $ ORACLE_HOME /rdbms/admin*

We can also create our own plan table with different name by altering the script utlxplan.sql.

The structure of the table **PLAN_TABLE** is like,

| COLUMN NAME | DATA TYPE |
|---|---|
| STATEMENT_ID | VARCHAR2(30) |
| TIMESTAMP | DATE |
| REMARKS | VARCHAR2(80) |
| OPERATION | VARCHAR2(30) |
| OPTIONS | VARCHAR2(225) |
| OBJECT_NODE | VARCHAR2(128) |
| OBJECT_OWNER | VARCHAR2(30) |
| OBJECT_NAME | VARCHAR2(30) |
| OBJECT_INSTANCE | NUMERIC |
| OBJECT_TYPE | VARCHAR2(30) |
| OPTIMIZER | VARCHAR2(225) |
| SEARCH_COLUMNS | NUMBER |
| ID | NUMERIC |
| PARENT_ID | NUMERIC |
| POSITION | NUMERIC |
| COST | NUMERIC |
| CARDINALITY | NUMERIC |
| BYTES | NUMERIC |
| OTHER_TAG | VARCHAR2(225) |
| PARTITION_START | VARCHAR2(225) |
| PARTITION_STOP | VARCHAR2(225) |
| PARTITION_ID | NUMERIC |
| OTHER | LONG |
| DISTRIBUTION | VARCHAR2(30) |
| CPU_COST | NUMERIC |
| IO_COST | NUMERIC |
| TEMP_SPACE | NUMERIC |
| ACCESS_PREDICATES | VARCHAR2(4000) |
| FILTER_PREDICATES | VARCHAR2(4000) |

## Explain plan command

The EXPLAIN PLAN command is used to get the execution plan for a statement. The structure of the EXPLAIN PLAN is,

**Syntax:**

*EXPLAIN PLAN [SET STATEMETN_ID = 'TEXT' INTO PLAN TABLE]*
*FOR Sql Statement*

TEXT: Any valid text for statement id
PLAN TABLE: The plan table name, by default it is PLAN_TABLE
STATEMETN: Any valid sql statement

**Example:**

> *EXPLAIN PLAN FOR*
> > *Select * from emp;*

The above statement will insert a row in the plan table.

## Review the execution plan

The following factors are useful to examine the execution plan.

1. Check the deriving table is placed in the correct place
2. Check the join order, the join order should be in such a way that, each step in the join order should return the minimum number of rows to the next level.
3. Check whether the joining method is appropriate for the number of rows returned. For instance, nested loop join is not efficient when returning large number of rows
4. Check whether the views are used efficiently. Oracle will execute the views in different way than normal sql.
5. Check for the Cartesian products and try to avoid it if possible.
6. Analyze the sql statement whether the full table scan is efficient then indexes.

There are two script utilities used to display the EXPLAIN PLAN using the dbms_xplan package.

1. **utlxpls.sql:** This script used to display the explain plan for the last explained statement.

The query used is:

*SELECT plan_table_output*
*FROM TABLE (dbms_xplan.display('plan_table',null, 'serial'));*

2. **utlxplp**.sql: This script used to display the Parallel Query information if the plan happens to run parallel

The query used is,

*SELECT ***
 *FROM TABLE (dbms_xplan.display());*

# SQL Trace and TKPROF

The SQL Trace facility and TKPROF lets you accurately assess the efficiency of the SQL statements when an application runs. Although Explain plan is good for checking the cost of an SQL and helps in tuning the query, Oracle trace gives them a proper understanding and lets you know the efficiency of the SQL query.

The SQL Trace facility provides performance information on individual SQL statements. It generates the following statistics for each statement:

## Parse, execute, and fetch counts

- **Parse**: Whenever a SQL statement is executed, Oracle checks statement in terms of syntax, validity of objects being referred and privileges of the user. Oracle also checks for the identical statements that may have been fired, in order to reduce the processing time. All this takes place in a fraction of a second without the knowledge of the user. This process is known as **Parsing**.
  In case of trace parse tells us the no of times the SQL query is parsed before execution. Ideally it should be always be one.

- **Execute**: It gives the actual number of execution the SQL statement goes through in Oracle. For SELECT statements, this identifies the number of rows selected by query.

- **Fetch**: It gives the number of rows of data from the result set of a multi-row query. Fetches are only performed for SELECT queries.

1. CPU and elapsed times
2. Number of rows processed
3. Misses on the library cache
4. Username under which each parse occurred

We can enable the SQL Trace facility for a session or for an instance. When the SQL Trace facility is enabled, performance statistics for all SQL statements executed in a user session or in the instance are placed into trace files.

## Steps for Oracle Trace

- You will have to set trace on for the session

```
ALTER SESSION SET SQL_TRACE = TRUE;
```

- Identify the SPID for the session
- Execute the procedure or SQL Statement
- Alter the session to disable trace

> *ALTER SESSION SET SQL_TRACE = FALSE;*

- The trace file will be created with spid in the file name in the oracle server log file, use the below query to identify the path

> *select value from v$parameter where name = 'user_dump_dest';*

- We will not have read access in the directory; we will have to request Oracle DBA to get the file.
- The trace file as itself is not much readable, we will have to request Oracle DBA to run TKPROF on it and send the processed file to us.

## Sample Output in the trace file

Below is some sample output retrieved from the trace file.

| call | count | cpu | elapsed | disk | query | current | rows |
|------|-------|------|---------|------|-------|---------|------|
| Parse | 1 | 0.01 | 0.64 | 0 | 0 | 0 | 0 |
| Execute | 2995 | 0.15 | 0.78 | 0 | 0 | 0 | 0 |
| Fetch | 5990 | 3.27 | 50.12 | 4931 | 89837 | 0 | 2995 |
| total | 8986 | 3.43 | 51.54 | 4931 | 89837 | 0 | 2995 |

*Misses in library cache during parse: 1*
*Optimizer goal: CHOOSE*
*Parsing user id: 102     (recursive depth: 1)*

## Explanations of Important terminologies used in the Trace file

**Count:** This column tells us the number of times the PL/SQL statement was parsed, executed, or fetched.

**CPU:** This column gives the total CPU time in seconds for the all parse, execute, or fetch calls in the PL/SQL statement.

**Elapsed:** This column gives the total elapsed time in seconds

**Disk:** It shows the total number of data blocks physically read from the data files on disk.

**Query:** This column shows the total number of buffers retrieved in consistent mode.

**Rows:** This column gives the total number of the processed rows.

The conclusion that we can gather from the above trace data is that:

- Whenever the procedure (containing the given query) is executed, the above query is parsed only once (hence count as 1) and is stored in Oracle memory thus reducing processing overheads.
- The query was executed 2995 times due to recursive calls from within the procedure which took a CPU time of 0.15 seconds and physical time taken was 0.78 seconds.
- The query fetched a total of 5990 records of data which after proper combination resulted in 2995 rows of actual required data. This is in sync with count number from execute row .i.e. for each execution of the query a final single row of data was the output. The total CPU time for this fetch process was 3.27 seconds and the total physical time taken was 50.12 seconds. The total number of data blocks physically read from the disk was 4931.
- In a nutshell the given query in the example took a total of 51.54 seconds of physical time and 3.43 seconds of CPU time from the total time in which the procedure was completed say 200 seconds of physical time.
- There was in total 1 miss in library cache during query parsing.

The deciding factor after seeing the trace file is that to figure out which SQL needs to be tuned. We need to find those SQL statements which use most of the CPU or disk resource utilized.

If it is acceptable to have (say) 3.43 CPU seconds and to retrieve 2995 rows, then we don't need to look any further at the trace output. In fact, a major use of TKPROF reports in a tuning exercise is to eliminate processes from the detailed tuning phase.

## Why Use Oracle Trace

Now the question is that we can also use explain plan for tuning the SQL queries, then why should one go for Oracle trace rather that explain plan.

Assume that we are working with a package/procedure which has more than 30 SQL queries used in cursors. Then checking the performance of all those queries with the help of explain plan is cumbersome.
Secondly, pinpointing the exact problematic query will also be difficult. Taking Oracle trace into consideration, we would only need to the SQL_TRACE to true and then need to run the package/procedure. After the process is complete set the SQL_TRACE to false and ask the Oracle

DBA to run TKPROF on the output file and then provide that to us. That single file would contain the details for each and every SQL statements that is present in the object that was executed (like the one shown in the above example) thus making the process much simpler and faster.

Hence by just looking at the CPU/Elapsed timings we can pinpoint the problematic query. The best results can be obtained by using the output of trace file with Oracle Explain Plan.

# SQL Analytical Functions

Analytical functions are used to do many things which we cannot do directly with WHERE clause like, Calculate a running total", "Find percentages within a group", "Top-N queries", "Compute a moving average" and many more.

Analytical functions used to compute aggregate values based on certain group of rows.

This group of rows is called "window" defined by the analytical clause. Analytical functions are the last set of functions executed in the WHERE clause.

**Syntax:**

*Analytic_function(arguments)*
*Over (<Partition by clause>*
*<order by clause>*
*<windowing clause>*
*)*

Some of the functions are:
Rank, dense rank, row number, etc.

Consider the following examples,

*Running Total*

```
SQL> break on deptno skip 1
SQL>SELECT d.deptno, d.dname, e.empno, e.ename, sal,
        SUM (e.sal) OVER (ORDER BY d.deptno, e.ename) "running total",
        SUM (e.sal) OVER (PARTITION BY d.deptno ORDER BY e.empno) "dept total",
        ROW_NUMBER () OVER (PARTITION BY d.deptno ORDER BY e.ename) "sequence"
    FROM scott.emp e, scott.dept d
    where d.deptno in (10,20);
```

| DEPTNO | DNAME | EMPNO | ENAME | SAL | running total | dept total | sequence |
|---|---|---|---|---|---|---|---|
| 10 | ACCOUNTING | 7876 | ADAMS | 1100 | 1100 | 23775 | 1 |
| | ACCOUNTING | 7499 | ALLEN | 1600 | 2700 | 2400 | 2 |
| | ACCOUNTING | 7698 | BLAKE | 2850 | 5550 | 10725 | 3 |
| | ACCOUNTING | 7782 | CLARK | 2450 | 8000 | 13175 | 4 |
| | ACCOUNTING | 7902 | FORD | 3000 | 11000 | 27725 | 5 |
| | ACCOUNTING | 7900 | JAMES | 950 | 11950 | 24725 | 6 |
| | ACCOUNTING | 7566 | JONES | 2975 | 14925 | 6625 | 7 |
| | ACCOUNTING | 7839 | KING | 5000 | 19925 | 21175 | 8 |
| | ACCOUNTING | 7654 | MARTIN | 1250 | 21175 | 7875 | 9 |
| | ACCOUNTING | 7934 | MILLER | 1300 | 22475 | 29025 | 10 |
| | ACCOUNTING | 7788 | SCOTT | 3000 | 25475 | 16175 | 11 |
| | ACCOUNTING | 7369 | SMITH | 800 | 26275 | 800 | 12 |
| | ACCOUNTING | 7844 | TURNER | 1500 | 27775 | 22675 | 13 |
| | ACCOUNTING | 7521 | WARD | 1250 | 29025 | 3650 | 14 |
| 20 | RESEARCH | 7876 | ADAMS | 1100 | 30125 | 23775 | 1 |
| | RESEARCH | 7499 | ALLEN | 1600 | 31725 | 2400 | 2 |
| | RESEARCH | 7698 | BLAKE | 2850 | 34575 | 10725 | 3 |
| | RESEARCH | 7782 | CLARK | 2450 | 37025 | 13175 | 4 |
| | RESEARCH | 7902 | FORD | 3000 | 40025 | 27725 | 5 |
| | RESEARCH | 7900 | JAMES | 950 | 40975 | 24725 | 6 |
| | RESEARCH | 7566 | JONES | 2975 | 43950 | 6625 | 7 |
| | RESEARCH | 7839 | KING | 5000 | 48950 | 21175 | 8 |
| | RESEARCH | 7654 | MARTIN | 1250 | 50200 | 7875 | 9 |
| | RESEARCH | 7934 | MILLER | 1300 | 51500 | 29025 | 10 |
| | RESEARCH | 7788 | SCOTT | 3000 | 54500 | 16175 | 11 |
| | RESEARCH | 7369 | SMITH | 800 | 55300 | 800 | 12 |
| | RESEARCH | 7844 | TURNER | 1500 | 56800 | 22675 | 13 |
| | RESEARCH | 7521 | WARD | 1250 | 58050 | 3650 | 14 |

```
28 rows selected.
```

- The ORDER BY clause in the over () will order the rows and then calculate the sum.
- The PARTITION BY clause in the over () will divide the row sets based on the partition key and then calculate the sum
- The ROW_NUMBER () will populate the sequence number either of all the rows or for each partition set of rows.

## Top- N rows

```
SQL> break on dname skip 1
SQL> SELECT *
    FROM (SELECT d.dname, e.empno, e.ename, e.sal,
              ROW_NUMBER () OVER (PARTITION BY d.deptno ORDER BY sal desc) top3
        FROM scott.emp e, scott.dept d
      WHERE d.deptno = e.deptno)
    WHERE top3 <= 3;

DNAME                 EMPNO ENAME              SAL      TOP3
---------------   --------- ----------   ---------   --------
ACCOUNTING             7934 MILLER            1300         1
                       7782 CLARK             2450         2
                       7839 KING              5000         3

RESEARCH               7369 SMITH              800         1
                       7876 ADAMS             1100         2
                       7566 JONES             2975         3

SALES                  7900 JAMES              950         1
                       7521 WARD              1250         2
                       7654 MARTIN            1250         3

9 rows selected.
```

In the above example the POW_NUMBER () can only put the sequence of numbers to identify the sequence of the rows.

## Rank the Row

```
SQL>   select * from (select d.dname, e.empno, e.ename, e.sal,
  2              rank () OVER (PARTITION BY d.deptno ORDER BY sal desc) top3
  3            FROM scott.emp e, scott.dept d
  4          WHERE d.deptno = e.deptno)
  5    WHERE top3 <= 3;

DNAME                 EMPNO ENAME              SAL      TOP3
---------------   --------- ----------   ---------   --------
ACCOUNTING             7839 KING              5000         1
                       7782 CLARK             2450         2
                       7934 MILLER            1300         3

RESEARCH               7788 SCOTT             3000         1     ----
                       7902 FORD              3000         1     ----
                       7566 JONES             2975         3

SALES                  7698 BLAKE             2850         1
                       7499 ALLEN             1600         2
                       7844 TURNER            1500         3

9 rows selected.
```

The RANK () function will rank the key field. Rows with equal values for the ranking criteria receive the same rank. When two values gets the same rank then it will skip the next consecutive rank. See the above example.

## Dense Ranking

```
SQL> SELECT *
  2     FROM (SELECT d.dname, e.empno, e.ename, e.sal,
  3                  DENSE_RANK () OVER (PARTITION BY d.deptno ORDER BY sal DESC)
  4                                                                          top3
  5            FROM scott.emp e, scott.dept d
  6           WHERE d.deptno = e.deptno)
  7     WHERE top3 <= 3;

DNAME              EMPNO ENAME           SAL    TOP3
---------------    ----- ---------    -------   -----
ACCOUNTING          7839 KING          5000      1
                    7782 CLARK         2450      2
                    7934 MILLER        1300      3

RESEARCH            7788 SCOTT         3000      1    ---
                    7902 FORD          3000      1    ---
                    7566 JONES         2975      2    ---
                    7876 ADAMS         1100      3

SALES               7698 BLAKE         2850      1
                    7499 ALLEN         1600      2
                    7844 TURNER        1500      3

10 rows selected.
```

Dense rank will not skip the value when two or more values get same rank.

## Range and Rows

The RANGE option is used to collect a set of rows based on the given range and then works for it. If I say RANGE 5 PRECEDING then it will get 5 values preceding the current row and then works for it like count the rows or find average, etc.,

Consider the following example.

```
SQL> SELECT     ename, hiredate, hiredate - 100 hiredate_pre,
  2                 COUNT (*) OVER (ORDER BY hiredate ASC RANGE 100 PRECEDING) cnt
  3          FROM scott.emp
  4    ORDER BY hiredate ASC;

ENAME      HIREDATE    HIREDATE_       CNT
---------- ----------- -----------  ---------
SMITH      17-DEC-80   08-SEP-80        1
ALLEN      20-FEB-81   12-NOV-80        2
WARD       22-FEB-81   14-NOV-80        3
JONES      02-APR-81   23-DEC-80        3    ---
BLAKE      01-MAY-81   21-JAN-81        4    ---
CLARK      09-JUN-81   01-MAR-81        3    ---
TURNER     08-SEP-81   31-MAY-81        2
MARTIN     28-SEP-81   20-JUN-81        2
KING       17-NOV-81   09-AUG-81        3
JAMES      03-DEC-81   25-AUG-81        5
FORD       03-DEC-81   25-AUG-81        5
MILLER     23-JAN-82   15-OCT-81        4
SCOTT      09-DEC-82   31-AUG-82        1
ADAMS      12-JAN-83   04-OCT-82        2

14 rows selected.
```

The above example shows number of employees hired in 100 days interval.
The RANGE will work find for numeric and date.

The ROWS also will work in the same manner. Consider the following example,

```
SQL> SELECT     deptno "Deptno", ename "Ename", sal "Sal",
  2                 SUM (sal) OVER (PARTITION BY deptno ORDER BY ename ROWS 2 PRECEDING) "Sliding Total"
  3          FROM scott.emp
  4    ORDER BY deptno, ename;

Deptno Ename         Sal Sliding Total
------ ---------- ------ -------------
    10 CLARK        2450         2450
       KING         5000         7450
       MILLER       1300         8750

    20 ADAMS        1100         1100
       FORD         3000         4100
       JONES        2975--       7075
       SCOTT        3000--       8975
       SMITH         800--       6775

    30 ALLEN        1600         1600
       BLAKE        2850         4450
       JAMES         950         5400
       MARTIN       1250         5050
       TURNER       1500         3700
       WARD         1250         4000

14 rows selected.
```

### First Value and Last Value

The first row and the last row functions used to get the first and last value based on the given criteria.

```
SQL> break on deptno skip 1
SQL> SELECT    deptno, ename, sal,
  2             FIRST_VALUE (ename) OVER (PARTITION BY deptno ORDER BY sal ASC) AS min_sal_has
  3       FROM scott.emp
  4  ORDER BY deptno,sal;

   DEPTNO ENAME             SAL MIN_SAL_HA
   ------ ---------- ---------- ----------
       10 MILLER           1300 MILLER
          CLARK            2450 MILLER
          KING             5000 MILLER

       20 SMITH             800 SMITH
          ADAMS            1100 SMITH
          JONES            2975 SMITH
          FORD             3000 SMITH
          SCOTT            3000 SMITH

       30 JAMES             950 JAMES
          MARTIN           1250 JAMES
          WARD             1250 JAMES
          TURNER           1500 JAMES
          ALLEN            1600 JAMES
          BLAKE            2850 JAMES

14 rows selected.
```

In the above example, the last column shows the first low salary person in each department. The last value function also will work in the same manner.

## LAG

The LAG provides access to more than one row prior to the current row in a table at the same time without self-join.

**Syntax:**

*LAG (value_expr [, offset] [, default])*
   *OVER ([partition-clause] order-by-clause)*

**Value_expr:** The column name based on which the LAG work
**Offset:** The number of prior value access to the LAG
**Default:** Provides default value when the offset goes beyond the window.

Consider the following example,

```
SQL> SELECT ename, hiredate, sal,
  2          LAG (sal, 1, 0) OVER (ORDER BY hiredate) AS prevsal
  3     FROM scott.emp
  4    WHERE deptno = 10;

ENAME      HIREDATE      SAL  PREVSAL
---------- ---------- ------ --------
CLARK      09-JUN-81    2450        0
KING       17-NOV-81    5000     2450
MILLER     23-JAN-82    1300     5000
```

The above example shows the salary just before the current hiring salary.

## LEAD

The LEAD provides access to more than one row next to the current row in a table at the same time without self-join.

**Syntax:**

*LEAD (value_expr [, offset] [, default])*
   *OVER ([partition-clause] order-by-clause)*

**Value_expr:** The column name based on which the LEAD work
**Offset:** The number of prior value access to the LEAD
**Default:** Provides default value when the offset goes beyond the window.

Consider the following example,

```
SQL> SELECT ename, hiredate,
  2         LEAD (hiredate, 1) OVER (ORDER BY hiredate) AS nexthired
  3    FROM scott.emp
  4   WHERE deptno = 10;

ENAME      HIREDATE   NEXTHIRED
---------  ---------  ---------
CLARK      09-JUN-81  17-NOV-81
KING       17-NOV-81  23-JAN-82
MILLER     23-JAN-82
```

The above example shows the hire date just after the current hire date.

# Performance Tuning of PL/SQL Code

## What is PL/SQL?

PL/SQL is a procedural language that has both interactive SQL and procedural programming language constructs such as iteration, branching, nesting etc. PL/SQL uses block structure. A block is a set of related declarations and procedural statements. The components of a PL/SQL block are as given below:

DECLARE

/* Declarative Part */

BEGIN

/* Executable part */

EXCEPTION

/* Exception handling Part */

END;

## Difference between SQL and PL/SQL

| SQL | PL/SQL |
|---|---|
| It's a non-procedural language | It's a procedural language wherein a list of operations can be performed sequentially |
| Here queries are used to access the database | It uses variables, functions, procedures etc |
| No looping can be done through records | Looping is possible through records, processing them one by one |
| A SQL statement is a specific instance of a valid SQL command. | Several SQL commands can be grouped to form stored procedures to achieve the desired result. |

| Exceptions cannot be handled | Exceptions can be handled effectively |
|---|---|

## What is PL/SQL Tuning?

Tuning PL/SQL programs in general make the application database run faster leading to higher efficiency. Tuning becomes necessary when too many resources are used and it is hampering the performance. PL/SQL tuning takes into account the frequency of accessing database, memory utilization, database availability etc.

## When to tune PL/SQL

PL/SQL tuning can be done when:

- Old programs are to be optimized which hadn't taken advantage of PL/SQL features.

- Programs that do multiple INSERT, DELETE, UPDATE statements and looping through query results.

- Programs requiring lot of mathematical calculations wherein the data types are to be further investigated.

- Sub functions that are invoked from within queries which are to be executed millions of times.

## Why PL/SQL Tuning is done?

There are mainly three reasons for a PL/SQL stored procedure hampering the performance:

- High Communication overhead – In a networked environment, the SQL statements sent over the network can lead to increased traffic which may raise the overhead.

- Inefficient SQL Statements – Time consuming SQL statements fired can affect performance of the entire stored procedure.

- Unwanted parsing and binding – Improper management of cursors used in the procedure can lead to unnecessary parsing and binding.

Parsing is the process of validation of syntax rules and binding means associating the host variables with their addresses.

PL/SQL tuning mainly refers to the process of ensuring that the SQL statements fired within the stored procedure would run as fast as possible.

## Use FORALL and BULK COLLECT

The PL/SQL features FORALL and BULK COLLECT improve the performance of PL/SQL code significantly. If the code contains SQL statements like INSERT, UPDATE, and DELETE in a PL/SQL loop, replace the normal FOR LOOP, and WHILE loops with FORALL for executing INSERT, UPDATE, and DELETE will gives significant results. This will reduce the context switches between PL/SQL and SQL Engines.

For looping through the result set of SELECT query use BULK COLLECT clause of SELECT INTO to bring entire result set into memory using single context switch.

## Use NOCOPY compiler hint

Whenever you need to pass parameters to sub programs in PL/SQL by default OUT, IN OUT parameters passed by value. Before execution of subprogram parameter values are copied and written back as soon as sub program execution completes successfully. If any error occurs during the execution of subprograms, the original value will not change. If the parameters are collections, records or object instances with large volumes of data the copying process may slow down the execution. To fix this performance issue you can use NOCOPY hint to enforce the passing data by reference. You need to have complete exception handling in the subprogram as an exception in the subprogram may destroy the original data.

## Use Native dynamic SQL with EXECUTE IMMEDIATE in place of DBMS_SQL

In some PL/SQL programs you may need to execute code unavailable in PL/SQL, e.g. DDL statements, or to generate DCL statements dynamically. Use Dynamic SQL statements to execute these kinds of statements. Previously it was available using DBMS_SQL package. However, nowadays Oracle recommends using Dynamic SQL as it is more compact and efficient.

PL/SQL provides two different kinds of statements in support of Dynamic SQL statements. The first one is EXECUTE IMMEDIATE, used to execute DDL, DCL, or any DML statement from PL/SQL code. The other one, called BULK BINDING is used for performing multi row queries is OPEN-FOR, FETCH, and CLOSE statements.

Dynamic SQL statement can include the following

- SELECT, INSERT, DELETE, and UPDATE

- PL/SQL blocks

- DDL/DCL (COMMIT, ROLLBACK, or SAVEPOINT) statements

- Session control statements

## Why is Dynamic SQL faster than DBMS_SQL?

Native dynamic SQL bundles statement preparation, binding, and execution steps into one operation. Native dynamic SQL has PL/SQL built in support. Use Bind variables with Native dynamic SQL which also helps in improving the performance as Oracle shares a single cursor for multiple SQL statements. Native SQL requires less coding when compared to DBMS_SQL as preparation, binding, and execution in a single step whereas DBMS_SQL has different procedures for parsing, binding, execution, and close of cursor.

## How does Oracle PL/SQL Optimization works in 10G?

Performance of PL/SQL code improved with new changes to the Optimizer in 10G. By default all the performance improvements are automatic. Oracle introduced the PLSQL_OPTIMIZE_LEVEL parameter first time in 10G. This explains the optimization level that will be used to compile PL/SQL library units. The higher the setting of this parameter, the more effort the compiler takes to tune PL/SQL units. This parameter can have one of the following values:

- **Value 0** – No optimization.

- **Value 1** – This brings minor optimization. This will take out unnecessary exceptions and computations. It does not move source code out of its original source order. If you see some exceptions not raised or behaving differently than change this value to 0.

- **Value 2** – This is the default optimization in Oracle 10G. This includes Level 1 changes and code rewrites for significant performance. If any large PL/SQL applications take a long time to compile then switch this value to 1. If the value is set to 2 optimizer behaves intelligently and rewrites and rearranges the code.

You can verify the values of PLSQL_OPTIMIZE_LEVEL in the view ALL_PLSQL_OBJECT_SETTINGS

# SQL Tips and Tricks

1. Use views as much as possible.

2. Avoid Cartesian products.

3. Avoid the full table scan when a query results less number of rows in a large table and go for full table scan when a query returns large number of rows from a large table.

4. Try to avoid full table scans using index.

5. Try to avoid using functions on indexed column in the sql statements.

6. Use the sql functions on the right side of the where clause instead of using the same on the indexed columns.

7. Try to write separate small sql statements.

8. Driving table is the table containing the filter conditions that eliminate the highest percentage of table/ records. These tables should be joined first.

9. If a view is defined on 2 or more base tables then don't use the view when you don't need the columns from both the tables. If a column from a single table is used then use the base table instead.

10. Use of materialized view is preferred as they store the pre computed/ aggregated results.

11. Use partioning on tables.

12. Use case statements to avoid multiple scans of same table.

13. Use equijoins whenever possible instead of inequality joins.

14. "IN" is more beneficial when most selective predicate (where predicate clause which returns lesser number of rows) is in the sub query i.e. use in when the sub query returns less number of rows.

15. "EXISTS" is more beneficial when most selective predicate (where clause which returns lesser number of rows) is in the parent query i.e. use in when the parent query returns less number of rows.

16. If select statement is trying to select less than or equal to around 10% of rows then it is better to use index scan otherwise use full scan for large tables.

17. Mostly used columns in WHERE, ORDER BY, and GROUP BY clauses, should be indexed. It gives better performance of the SQL query.

18. Temp tables (including materialize clause) are useful when using the same dataset many times in join of many tables.

19. Use triggers only whenever required. Row level triggers are very dangerous mainly.

20. Use BULK COLLECT in large number of data transactions.

21. PIN frequently used stored procedures in the SGA using the Oracle supplied package DBMS_SHARED_POOL.

22. Keep most frequently used lookup tables in the database buffer cache using BUFFER_POOL KEEP in the Create table syntax.

23. Use hints if you want to override indexes used by cost based optimization
    */*+ index (table_name index_name) */*

24. Use hints to change optimizer goal to rule if you are not satisfied with cost based optimization.
    */*+ optimizer_goal rule */*

25. When the code/query is compiling correctly then only we should go for tuning.

26. Whenever there is use of more than one tables always use table aliases and also prefix column names by their aliases. This will result in reduced parse time and will prevent future syntax errors like (ORA-00918: COLUMN AMBIGUOUSLY DEFINED).

27. Always develop the query as simple as possible i.e. there should be no unnecessary columns selected, GROUP BY or ORDER BY.
    Use:
    *SELECT supplier_id, last_name, first_name, address, state FROM supplier;*
    *Rather than,*
    *SELECT * FROM supplier;*

28. There are many WHERE clauses which do not use indexes at all. Oracle will ignore the index even if there is an index present over a column that is referenced by a WHERE clause. In single word, Never perform operations on objects referenced in the WHERE clause:
    Use:
    *SELECT client_name, org_date, amount FROM pre_sales WHERE amount > 0;*
    *Rather than:*
    *SELECT client_name, org_date, amount FROM pre_sales WHERE amount != 0;*

    ---

    Use:
    *SELECT acct_name, txn_date, amount FROM txn WHERE acct_name **LIKE 'BOLD%'**;*
    *Rather than:*

*SELECT acct_name, txn_date, amount FROM txn WHERE*
**SUBSTR(acct_name,1,4)**=*'BOLD';*

29. Never use a HAVING clause in SELECT statements. The issue with HAVING clause is that it filters rows only after all rows have been retrieved. WHERE clause will help in reducing overheads in summing, sorting etc.
    Use:
    *SELECT state FROM india* **WHERE** *state!= 'Rajasthan' AND state!= 'Gujarat';*
    *GROUP BY state;*
    Rather than:
    *SELECT state FROM india GROUP BY state* **HAVING** *state!= 'Rajasthan' AND state!= 'Gujarat';*

30. Always seek to reduce the number of subquery blocks in queries
    Use:
    *SELECT name FROM staff WHERE* **(staff_category, sal)** = **(SELECT** *MAX(category), MAX(sal) FROM staff_categories) AND staff_dept = 0029;*
    Rather than:
    *SELECT name FROM staff WHERE* **staff_category**=**(SELECT** *MAX(category) FROM staff_categories) AND* **staff_range** = **(SELECT** *MAX(sal) FROM staff_categories) AND staff_dept = 0020;*

31. We should consider the benefits for each (EXISTS, IN and table joins) when we are doing multiple table joins. It all depends on data one or other may be faster.
    → IN is considered the slowest.
    → IN will be more efficient when most of the filters are in the sub-query; and also EXISTS will be more efficient when most of the filters are in the parent-query.

32. EXISTS is a better alternative than DISTINCT to avoid full table scan as DISTINCT will cause Oracle to get all rows meeting the requirements of table join and then will do the sorting and filtering out of duplicate values. As in case of EXISTS, the Oracle optimizer gets to know when the subquery has been satisfied once, then there is no need to continue further and the next matching row can be get.
    Use:
    *SELECT L.id, L.description FROM large_table L WHERE* **EXISTS** *(SELECT NULL FROM verylarge_table VL WHERE VL.id = L.id);*
    Rather than:
    *SELECT* **DISTINCT L.id, L.description** *FROM large_table L, verylarge_table VL WHERE L.id = VL.id;*

33. If you are using a column in a mathematical expression it's always advisable to put the column on one side of operator and all other values on the other. Non-column expressions are most often handled earlier thereby boosting the query.
    Use:
    *WHERE AMOUNT < 100/(1 - n);*
    Rather than:
    *WHERE AMOUNT - (n * AMOUNT) < 100;*

34. DECODE is an applicable function used to bypass having to scan ditto rows repetitively or merge the equivalent table repetitively.
USE:
*SELECT COUNT(**DECODE**(flag, 'Yes', 'Z',NULL)) count_Y,*
*COUNT(**DECODE**(flag, 'No', 'Z',NULL)) count_N*
*FROM cust WHERE cust_name LIKE 'DANIEL%';*
Raher than:
*SELECT COUNT(\*) FROM cust WHERE flag = 'Yes' AND cust_name LIKE 'DANIEL%';*

---

*SELECT COUNT(\*) FROM cust WHERE flag = 'No' AND cust_name LIKE 'DANIEL%';*

35. Always avert using functions on columns which are indexed unless a function-based index is already created; as it edges to full table scan although index is present on the column.

www.ingramcontent.com/pod-product-compliance
Lightning Source LLC
Chambersburg PA
CBHW060932050326
40689CB00013B/3060